Why Not Desserts?

with

Jeannette Werle

ISBN: 978-0-578-70249-0

This book is for educational purposes and not intended to diagnose, cure any disease, or replace the advice of your doctor. The author and publisher of this baking book are not responsible in any manner whatsoever for any adverse effects arising directly as a result of the information provided in this book.

Printed in USA

First published in 2020 by Amazon Publishing

Book cover design: Mayfly Design

Book page formatting: Word-2-Kindle

Photos of Bob's Red Mill products and store: Bob's Red Mill, reprinted with permission

Photos inside book: Jeannette Werle, unless indicated with photos inside book

Cover: KDP-Amazon. Kindle Direct Publishing

This book is dedicated to my husband for his unwavering support of my many endeavors. You stood by me offering your support when I did not think I could continue. I love you.

Table of Contents

Pair the tart dough of choice with the lemon curd. Photo shows Pâte Sablée dough.

My Story

In my childhood, I developed a love affair with all things baked. My paternal grandmother introduced me to this world. She was a wonderful from-scratch cook and home baker. Later in life, my own style of baking emerged through training at prestigious culinary schools inside and outside the United States. I was able to put all this training to use in my small bakery, which I opened in 1992 and sold in early February 2018. I am also a certified integrated health coach and a graduate of Institute for Integrative Nutrition in New York. You will find in this book many recipes that include alternative ingredients to help with dietary challenges as well as regular recipes.

I got into the alternative field of baking during the last 11 years of bakery ownership because I had a mom who used to stop at my market booth almost every Saturday. She would buy an 8" brown box full of European and American pastries, but she would always ask if I had anything dairy and gluten free. I would answer no, but I would say, "I can certainly bake them!" Well, this went on for a few weeks or maybe longer, until she introduced me to her son. The request had a face, a 10-year-old, thin, blond, well- mannered kid and the only one of four children who could not eat dairy or gluten in her family. I felt terrible! I could no longer keep telling her the same story, so this is how I developed a full bakery menu that had alternative pastries, cakes, cookies, donuts, and breads. By the time the bakery was sold, my sales from alternative baking were around 30 percent of the total sales, and it had grown by solid word of mouth. I even had referrals from a local hospital.

Another factor that contributed to my success in alternative baking is, at the age of 25, I lost the enzymes to digest dairy which forced me to adapt my cooking, baking, and diet to meet my health needs. Eventually, I was able to reintroduce dairy into my diet, but intermittently by choice. Hence the name of this book came from the fact, that supporting gut health more specifically the microbiome brings about the resolution of gut and other health issues.

This book is intended to be used by anyone who enjoys sinking their teeth into tasty pastries, whether they choose to eat regular pastries or are required to eat alternative pastries to maintain health. My hope is that you will be able to find something for most palates or dietary needs, and my goal is to be inclusive of as many people as I can. Leave no one behind!

Precision scale, proofing bread basket, French rolling pin, ring tart, off set spatula and seed/nut grinder.

Chapter One

How to Use This Book

- To use this book, please read the recipes at least twice before preparing any recipe.
- Make a shopping ingredients list.
- The ingredients listed should be at the suggested temperature.
- The quality of the ingredients is important for obtaining consistent results. Please use fresh and in-season fruits. Flours and grains should be whole, if possible, and free of preservatives. They should be grown and harvested free of pesticides as well. My number one source of grains and flours is Bob's Red Mill. This company really believes in delivering wholesome products using clean practices.
- Accuracy is everything in baking; weigh ingredients to be successful.
- If you have no scale, use volume cups and scoop the flour into the measuring cup by using a knife point to fill. Avoid tapping or packing the cup.
- Liquid measuring cups do not have the same capacity volume as dry measuring cups.
- Get familiar with baking terms. See glossary, p. 111

Legend:

P Paleo

GF Gluten Free

DF Dairy Free

NS No Sugar Added

LF Lactose Free

SCD Specific Carbohydrate Diet

RSF Refined Sugar Free

V Vegan

Wholesome Ingredients

The photos in this page were reprinted by permission from Bob's Red Mill.

The next time you're in Portland, Oregon, make time to visit the Bob's Red Mill store and plant because you'll be in for a treat. You'll get to see all the different grains available and much more.

A Word About Ingredients

Harvesting and buying locally will help support your environment and your gut!

I would like to welcome you into the world of knowing your food source and the quality of your food. You have the right to know where your food comes from and how it was processed.

How can you demand better quality food? You can do this with your money. Be selective where you shop. Try to buy seasonal foods, but, most importantly, support local markets and farmers to benefit the organisms in our gut. Nowadays, we are exposed to foods that have been chemically altered or genetically modified. I encourage you to make yourself aware of what food brands are keeping alive the pure and simple practices of growing and processing food. Please read the label. You'll be surprised to find that many wheat flours are not genetically modified in the United States, but they have been chemically modified. This chemical modification has the power to alter the ecosystem in your gut and has the potential to make you sick. As an example, the spraying of glyphosate before planting and spraying again 14 days prior to harvesting of wheat is permitted in the United States. Glyphosate has patents in the United States for medical use in humans too. Check out the US patents for the medical use of glyphosate (3-4, p. 110). Please be an informed consumer. The use of a chemical has an accumulative repercussion for our immune system. The liver cannot detox all these exposures, which leads to chronic disease.

There are other factors that determine the quality of the flour, and the miller has these choices: natural or chemical aging of the grains, extraction rates, tempering of bran, or mellowing the endosperm, among other practices. Some milling practices can cause grains to lose nutrients during the process. This is why many flours are enriched. This enrichment has no effect on the baking quality of the flour.

Bleaching of the flours is done to produce a natural-colored flour and a soft crumb in baking, but it also destroys the flour's natural carotenoid nutrients. Bleaching agents used include benzoyl peroxide, and chlorine gas is used to chemically age the flour (5 a,b,c, p. 110). Bleached flours are not good for breads because they produce a white and mellow-flavored bread. Potassium bromate and ascorbic acid are used to mature and age the flours, but they do not bleach. Some US states require disclosing to consumers that some ingredients are added during the processing of flour, and these can cause ill health effects.

Preservatives added to flours include calcium propanoate, sodium benzoate, tricalcium phosphate, and butylated hydroxyanisole.

Malting is used to treat wheat flours with the addition of malted barley flours. Malting aids in the conversion of starches to dextrins and into fermented sugar like maltose. The natural occurring yeast can then feed on the sugars, which helps it convert them into carbon dioxide (CO_2) and alcohol. Malt improves fermentation, crust color, and the volume of baked goods.

It is best to use organic grains if possible or, at least, grown without chemicals or pesticides. Try to use the whole grain to provide full nutrition to your body. Grains have three parts to them: the bran, the endosperm, and the germ. The endosperm contains proteins, starches, and water, the germ contains fats and micronutrients, and the bran is rich in fiber (cellulose) and minerals.

Common Wheat Unbleached Flours Available

- All-purpose flour – derived from hard or soft wheat, 10 to 12 grams of protein content
- Bread flour – wheat derived from hard wheat, 12 to 16 grams of protein content
- Cake flour – wheat derived, soft wheat, 7 to 9 grams of protein content
- Whole grain wheat flour – protein content of 16 grams of protein

Use the right protein content to achieve the right texture and consistency. Below is the formula for determining the protein content of your flour.

Package is marked with 34 g per serving (¼ cup), 4 g protein. What is the protein percentage of the flour? The answer is 11.7 % protein. This percentage is good for all-purpose flour jobs.

1. 4 grams of protein per serving of 34 grams of flour.
2. (4 g protein/34 g flour) x 100 = 11.7% protein in the flour

In general, there are many farmers and manufacturers that are responsible for the growth and processing of grains and foods. Please support them.

Non-grain and Gluten-Free Flours I Use (Seeds, Starches, and Nuts)

Almond flour, hazelnut flour, sunflower flour, pumpkin flour, arrowroot flour, plantain flour, cassava flour, and many others. For most of the nuts and seeds, I roast them first lightly and then grind them finely into flours.

Gluten-Free Flours

I bake with Bob's Red Mill flours and grains 98 percent of the time. Please see the supplies section.

Buckwheat, Millet, and Quinoa

These are technically seeds, not grains, and are rich in many micronutrients. Quinoa seeds need to be rinsed before cooking due to their coating, called saponin, a natural insect repellent coating. The saponin is said to bind to the mineral receptors of your cells, so rinsing the quinoa before cooking reduces this effect as well as removes the bitter flavor. Quinoa, like buckwheat, are considered whole proteins containing nine of the essential amino acids. They have many uses: buckwheat makes a great porridge, millet and quinoa can be used directly into salads, and when ground into a flour, they can be combined with other gluten-free seeds and grains to make great bread.

Sorghum

This is one of my favorite flours for baking breads, having a lovely light yellow color with sweet tones, while it produces dense breads. Sorghum is a gluten-free grass grain. It's loaded with many micronutrients, making it an ideal grain to replace wheat in a gluten-free diet. It can be popped like popcorn and cooked as a porridge.

Best Fats

Fats bring moisture, leavening, nutrition, flavor, and lubrication. Monounsaturated fats are healthy fats found in olives, avocados, and some nuts. They are considered heart healthy in moderation.

- *Unsalted butter* – from 100 percent grass-fed cows is best, a natural form of fat. Rich in vitamin D, A, and conjugated linoleic acid, a fatty acid found in grass-fed cows (9, p. 110). Butter in laminated doughs will provide a leavening action or creaming butter and sugar provides a lift to cakes.

- *Ghee* – milk solids are separated from the fat in a cooking process leaving the fat behind. It has a lovely nutty flavor and aroma. Ghee is paleo and SCD friendly. Some lactose-intolerant people can use this healthy fat. Individuals allergic to milk will not be able to use this fat due to possible milk traces.

- *Coconut oil* – best organic, raw. Not refined. Use with caution because it is a saturated fat. Limit consumption to less than 10 percent. Avoid if you have a problem absorbing fat or have gall bladder problems.

- *Coconut butter* – the whole coconut is used to make this butter, and it has a higher melting point. It is not good for baking in certain instances, but the taste is delicious. Limit consumption to less than 10 percent. Avoid if you have problems absorbing fats.

- *Olive oil* – cold pressed, organic is best, buy in dark glass bottles to prevent oxidation. Add a small amount of olive oil to a butter cake to increase moisture and delay staling.

- *Sunflower oil* – organic is best, cold process, no hexane or high heat processing.

- *Avocado oil* – cold processed, buy in dark glass bottles to prevent oxidation.

Sugars - when heated during baking, sugars caramelize, bring color, and add flavor to bake goods. Sugars also provide moisture and softness in baking. Listed below are some of the sugars used in this book:

- *Fructose* – occurs naturally in fruits, some vegetables, sugar cane, and honey. It's the sweetest of the sugars and one of the components of sucrose or table sugar.

- *Table sugar or granulated sugar* – this refers to sucrose, a disaccharide of glucose and fructose. The body hydrolyzes sucrose into glucose and fructose, and it is especially concentrated in sugar cane and sugar beets, which are used in commercial sugar making. The glycemic index is 55. If you are prediabetic or diabetic, it will make your blood glucose rise and possibly trigger higher insulin resistance and high cholesterol.

- *Raw honey* – an unrefined sugar that contains traces of healthy nutrients. It is a source of antioxidants and is a monosaccharide sugar that is absorbed by the body quickly. A small amount is okay, but too much can raise blood glucose. Combining cinnamon with honey may help lower the glycemic index of the honey and work synergistically with insulin in the cells. It's great for paleo or SCD diets. Manuka honey has healing properties, but I will not get into this honey in this book.

- *Stevia pure* – a natural sugar extracted from the leaves of the stevia plant, a member of the sunflower family. Stevia has a zero glycemic index and has antibacterial properties. Research has been done in animals using pure stevia in an alcohol base suspension to combat Lyme disease, with excellent results at removing the biofilm and killing the *Borrelia Burgdorferi* bacteria and the closely related bacteria *Borrelia mayonii* in the United States (6, p. 110). Read the label because some manufacturers mix the stevia with other ingredients. Choose plain stevia in a water or alcohol base or just dried leaves powder for best results.

- *Erythritol* – a natural sugar alcohol, but it is neither a sugar nor an alcohol. It is 60–70 percent as sweet as sucrose (table sugar), but it does not raise blood glucose like regular sugar does, and it has a glycemic index of 1. However, it has many side effects if consumed in large amounts: diarrhea, upset stomach, nausea, cramping, bloating, and headaches. This is because the bacteria in the colon cannot digest it. Erythritol is different from other sugar alcohols in that it gets absorbed by the body immediately, but 90 percent of it gets excreted unchanged. The other 10 percent arrives untouched, where the friendly bacteria in the gut are unable to break it down or digest it. This is the reason it causes digestive problems and bloating. Humans do not have the digestive enzymes needed to break down erythritol.

- *Yacón* – the yacón is a species of perennial daisy, traditionally grown in the northern and central Andes from Colombia to northern Argentina. It is sweet-tasting and has tuberous roots. The Yacón root is rich in prebiotic fiber fructo-oligosaccharides and inulin, and it can be used as a sweetener. There are some commercial brands that produce it in the United States that will not raise blood glucose. Yacón root is a prebiotic fiber that is food for the healthy bacteria in your colon. Yacón syrup can be used to replace honey, maple syrup, or molasses due to the syrup consistency being similar to the products listed here. Yacón is low glycemic index. See product resources for brand, p. 109.

Fruit Benefits

Fruits have many benefits: they are loaded with phytonutrients, fibers, and antioxidants that help remove and clean toxins out of the body, just like vegetable. Below I provide you with some of the benefits of the fruits I used in this book. Always use in-season, fresh fruit to obtain the most health benefits and best flavors.

- *Cherries* are loaded with phytonutrients, have antioxidant power, and may improve the cardiovascular system by reducing inflammation and lipid formation. Cherry juice may help promote better sleep by enhancing the body's production of melatonin. (10, p. 110).

  Other benefits of cherries are that they may help gout, macular degeneration, osteoarthritis, and blood circulation, and they are nutrient dense in minerals like potassium. Fresh cherries have a low glycemic fruit index of 22.

- *Apples* contain fibers, vitamin c, and phytochemicals (quercetin, anthocyanin, catechin, chlorogenic acid). Pectin is a soluble fiber that dissolves in water, forming a gel-like substance in the intestines. Pectin may help prevent constipation and is fermented in the colon by beneficial bacteria to form short-chain fatty acids. Short-chain fatty acids play a role in decrease inflammation, improve intestinal barrier, and may help in cancer prevention and other conditions. Apples also contain malic acid, which may help soften the liver and gallbladder stones, dilating the ducts of the gallbladder and liver, making the passage and elimination of the stones easier. The seeds contain a trace amount of cyanide, so avoid eating them. An interesting fact is that pectin binds to cholesterol in the digestive tract and slows glucose absorption by trapping carbohydrates.

- *Blueberries* are very popular due to the many medical studies showing that they are loaded with antioxidants and anti-inflammatory properties. Blueberries may be capable of preventing DNA damage, improving insulin resistance, and possibly reducing cardiovascular disease or damage. The phytochemicals (polyphenols) present in blueberries—anthocyanin (ANC), proanthocyanidin (PAC), and chlorogenic acid (CA)—are known to have beneficial health effects. When you cook blueberries or freeze them for a long time, these phytochemicals are lost or reduced. Fresh is best. Think of topping your dessert or breakfast with fresh, in-season blueberries.

Spices

Spices bring flavor, warmth, and sweet tones to cooking and baking, but in addition they have many health benefits. Listed below are some of the spices used in this book.

- *Cinnamon* adds warm and sweetness to baking, lowers blood glucose, may improve insulin sensitivity, may help fight bacterial and viral infections, is loaded with antioxidants, and is a good anti-inflammatory agent. It also may help fight against neurodegenerative diseases, inhibiting the buildup of a protein in the brain called Tau. Excessive Tau in the brain is a marker for Alzheimer's disease. Ceylon cinnamon is the only true cinnamon and it comes from Sri Lanka.

- *Turmeric* is used as a food color, brings warm flavors, and has antioxidant, anti-inflammatory, and antibacterial properties, and it improves brain function, preventing brain diseases. It may also lower the risk of heart disease.

- *Ginger* is closely related to turmeric, but it has spicy aromatic tones and is great for morning sickness, nausea, and upset stomachs. It has anti-inflammatory properties, and it can help reduce bad cholesterol (LDL), may reduce symptoms of irritable bowel syndrome, and may help protect against cancer.

- *Nigella sativa* – If you suffered or have in the past experienced a delayed or sudden food reaction, Nigella sativa oil might be of interest or help to you. The number one benefit I have experienced myself for food sensitivity relief comes from Nigella sativa oil. I'm talking relief within 10 to 30 min! I do not use it as an everyday supplement, but I do whenever I need support for my immune system. The top causes of food sensitivities are usually related to possible gut infections, autoimmune disorders, lack of proper stomach acid to digest foods, and purify them. To heal properly, the person will need to work on the root cause of the food sensitivities, but Nigella sativa can definitely help you quell the fire of a skin or systemic reaction within a short time. If you've ever had a skin reaction due to something you ate or touched, you know it is sudden, hot as fire, itchy, and leaves you frightened. Nigella sativa works by modulating the pathways between Th1 and Th2. In other words, it cools the skin reaction quickly by balancing the immune system (11, p. 110).

- Other benefits are immune modulators for autoimmune disorders, and it may reduce high blood pressure and help with sleep; hair loss; neurological disorders like anxiety, epilepsy, and Parkinson's; and viral, bacterial, fungal, and parasitic infections like malaria. It may also move the blood, helping improve oxygen and cell nutrition uptake, especially in cases of malnourished red blood cells. It also helps with skin conditions like eczema, psoriasis, inflammation, digestive issues, and pancreatitis.

- Dosage is based on weight and health conditions. The oil works the fastest and is best, but you can grind the seeds and add them to foods. I add the seeds to my homemade breads inside and as a topping, about ½ to 1 tsp. for extra nutrition. I have used the oil, but only as needed for one or two days.

> Please note that Nigella sativa is not for anaphylaxis reactions, a life-threatening allergic reaction, because it can close the airway, lower blood pressure, and cause vomiting or a weak pulse.
> Common triggers are foods like peanuts, latex, medications, and so on. If you are experiencing anaphylactic shock, call 9-11 and get immediate help.

Chapter Two

Tarts, Galette, and Cobbler

Lemon Curd Berry Tart

Strawberry Rhubarb Streusel Tart

Double Delight Cherry Tart

Strawberry Jam Tart

Fig Jam Tart

Chocolate Soufflé Wild Honey Raspberry Tart

Individual Savory Vegetable Galettes

Pumpkin Mousse Tart or Pie

Vanilla Apple Cobbler

Streusel Topping

Lemon Curd Berry Tart

GF, LF, RSF, Paleo

Lemon Curd Berry Tart

GF, LF, RSF, Paleo

Serves 6

Ingredients		
6, 3" Fully baked Almond Coconut tart shells, pg. 82	6	
Fresh lemon juice	4 oz.	½ Cup
Raw honey, mild flavor	5 oz.	½ Cup
Ghee, soft	3 oz.	
Gelatin plain	2 tsp.	
Water	1 tbsp.	
Egg yolks	4	
Celtic Salt	Pinch	
Pint fresh blueberries or meringue	1 pint	

Method:

Bloom the gelatin in 1 tbsp. cold water. Allow to rest for 10 min before using for the last stages of the lemon curd.

Cream the honey and ghee in a mixer for about 2–3 min.

Add egg yolks one a time and pinch salt.

Add lemon juice slowly until fully emulsified.

Transfer the lemon curd mixture to a nonreactive pot with a heavy bottom or, alternatively, cook it in a double-boiler until thick. The mixture should not boil but reach a temperature of 165 °F—or leave a path when a spoon is run on the side of the pot (nape).

Remove the cooked lemon curd from the heat, strain it, and immediately add the bloomed gelatin and mix thoroughly.

Store in the refrigerator, but cover the top with a layer of parchment paper to prevent a crust or drying.

Shelf life of lemon curd: five days.

Assemble Dessert: Divide the lemon curd among all six prebaked tart shells evenly and top with fresh berries or alternatively, top with a meringue instead of fruit. Serve immediately or prepare at least four hours in advance to prevent the crust from becoming soggy.

Baker's Tip:

Whisk the eggs one at a time quickly into the butter-sugar mixture because the sugar will burn the egg protein, causing egg clumps and a very acidic curd.

Strawberry Rhubarb Streusel Tart

Paleo, LF, GF, SF, Grain Free

Strawberry Rhubarb Streusel Tart

Paleo, LF, GF, SF, Grain Free

Serves 8

Ingredients filling		
10" Fully baked Almond Coconut tart shell, pg. 82	1	
Fresh Rhubarb diced	1 Cup	4.8 oz.
Fresh strawberries, quarter, first batch	2-1/2 Cup	16 oz.
Fresh lemon juice	2 tsp.	
Chia gel binder, pg. 86	¼ cup + 1 tbsp.	2.43 oz.
Stevia liquid	3/4 tsp.	
Cardamom ground	1 Pinch	
Celtic Salt	1 Pinch	
Fresh sliced strawberries, 2 batch	3 Cups	15 oz.

Streusel topping, p. 41, 1 batch

Method:

Prepare the streusel topping first and set it off to the side (p. 41). Preheat the oven to 350 °F.

In a small pot, place the washed diced rhubarb, first batch of quartered strawberries, chia gel, a pinch of salt, and cardamom. Cook it over a gentle heat covered for about 5 min until they are slightly tender and have sweat. Remove from the heat and add stevia and the second batch of sliced strawberries to the just cooked mixture. Toss until well mixed. Place the strawberry-rhubarb mixture into the just-baked almond coconut crust and top it with the streusel topping. Return the tart to the oven to bake for about 30 min until set and lightly golden brown. Once baked, remove it from the oven and place it on a wire rack to cool. When the tart is completely cool, remove it from the tart pan and transfer it to a display platter. This tart is best the day it is baked.

Baker's Tip:

The strawberry rhubarb filling is vegan. Optional: sprinkle cinnamon on top of the raw streusel just before baking.

Vegan option: Replace with vegan tart dough p. 83

Double Delight Cherry Tart

DF, GF, Paleo, Grain Free, SF

Growing and picking your own cherries early in the summer is a fun activity, and cherries are very nutrient dense. Bright red color all the way through in vegetables and fruits makes them rich in antioxidants (vitamin C). They also support heart and brain function, especially memory (See p. 19).

Top your baked filling with fresh pitted sweet cherries to retain the highest levels of nutrition.

Double Delight Cherry Tart

DF, GF, Paleo, Grain Free, RSF

This tart is made with sour cherries and sweet cherries that are cooked and baked as part of the filling and then crowned with many fresh pitted sweet cherries. The raw cherries are loaded with enzymes that aid in digestion and are loaded with antioxidants! We love cherries so much we grow them in our backyard.

Ingredients filling		
10" Fully baked grain free, tart shell, pg. 82	1	
Fresh sour cherries, pitted 1 batch	2-1/2 Cup	15 oz.
Fresh sweet cherries pitted, 1 batch, halved	2 Cups	15 oz.
Chia gel binder	½ Cup	5 oz.
Stevia liquid	1 tsp.	
Cardamom ground	1 Pinch	
Celtic Salt	1 Pinch	
Sweet Cherries, pitted	Garnish	1#

*Alternatively use Monk Fruit Sweetener.

Method:

Wash and pit the first batch of sweet cherries and sour cherries, place them in a medium pot with a pinch of Celtic salt and chia gel. Cook on low heat covered for about 5 min or until they sweat. Remove from the heat and add liquid stevia, cardamom and the halved sweet cherries. Place this filling into the baked tart and bake for about 30 min or until set. Remove from the oven and place on a wire rack until fully cool. Remove the tart from the pan and transfer it to a cake platter and top with extra sweet pitted cherries, about one pound. Serve the same day.

The photo below shows the baked filling.

Strawberry Jam Tart

Vegan option, Paleo, GF, NS

Strawberry Jam Tart

Vegan option, Paleo, GF, NS

This tart is best made in the spring and summer months when the strawberries are in season. They are very sweet and aromatic, so you will not need to add any glaze or extra sugar! Special equipment is needed, such as a 10" ring tart pan, ½" deep. This is a delicious summer dessert!

Serves 8

Ingredients filling		
10" Raw vegan tart shell, pg. 83	1	
or grain* free		
Strawberry fruit sweeten jam of choice, jar	1	9 oz.
Strawberries, fresh,	1	16 oz.

Method:

Wash the strawberries and take the crown offs. Leave the strawberries to dry on the counter over paper towels until needed. Set the raw tart shell ring over a tray lined with parchment paper. Bake the tart shell at 350 °F until golden brown and fully baked, especially in the center of the tart. Remove from the oven and immediately add the strawberry fruit sweetened jam to the bottom of the tart. Use an offset spatula to disperse evenly the contents of the store-bought jam over the bottom of the tart and bake an additional 10 to 15 min or until fully set and smooth. Remove from the oven and allow it to cool on the pan. Remove the tart ring and transfer the tart to a serving platter. Crown the top of the tart with the fresh strawberries. Serve the dessert the same day for the best taste.

Baker's Tip: Best results use a good quality fruit sweeten jam and make this tart with fresh spring or summer berries.

Fig Jam Tart

This is a variation of the strawberry jam tart. Use fresh mission figs. They are best when in season. I used strawberry jam sweetened fruit for the filling too, but, in this tart, I baked the figs on top of the jam to infuse the fl avors together. Prepare the fig tart following the instructions of the strawberry jam tart, but finish with the steps listed below.

Vegan, NS

Replace the strawberries with 1 ½ pound of fresh figs that have been washed and cut in half. Arrange them around the top of the strawberry jam and bake the tart with the fruit on top. Bake for 30 min at 350 F. Remove from the oven and allow it to cool completely before removing from the tart pan. It is best eaten the same day as baked, but it will last for about three days.

Chocolate Soufflé Wild Honey Raspberry Tart

Ingredients

10" round, par-baked Pate sable tart, 1-1/2-2", pg. 80	1	
Wild raw honey	1/4 Cup	2.5 oz.
Eggs large each	3	
Semi-sweet Belgian chocolate chips, melted		5 oz.
All-purpose flour	1/3 Cup, 1 tbsp.	oz.
Unsalted butter, melted	¼ Cup	2oz.
Hard ganache batch	1	
Raspberries fresh	1 pint	

Method:

The Soufflé, in a bain-marie (double boiler), melt the semisweet chocolate and unsalted butter. Mix well and set off to the side.

In a medium 4½ quart mixer bowl, whip the eggs until double in size and slowly add the wildflower honey to the whipped eggs. When the eggs have doubled, add the flour in a steady flow, mixing lightly. Remove from the mixer and fold in the melted chocolate-butter mixture in two to three batches until just combined. Remove the partially baked tart from the oven and fill with the chocolate soufflé mixture so it is just slightly under the top edge of the tart. Bake for about 10 min in a preheated oven at 350°F. The soufflé will set and look slightly dry to the touch. Avoid over baking or it will be dry and hard. Once baked, remove it from the oven to cool on a wire rack for about 10 min. Coat the tart with hard ganache and smooth the top and edges with an offset spatula. Let it rest in the tart shell pan until set, about 20 min. Top it with fresh raspberries and serve or store in the refrigerator until ready to serve. It has a shelf life of two days. It is best served warm.

Individual Savory Vegetable Galettes

Individual Savory Vegetable Galettes

These free-form tarts make a quick breakfast or lunch on the go. We sold many of these galettes in the bakery, filling them with apples, cherries, peaches, or savory fillings like vegetables and meat or just vegetables like the recipe below.

Pate Brisée dough	1 batch
Egg white for wash	1
Celtic Sat	1 pinch
Olive oil	
Fresh herbs of choice like basil, thyme	
Vegetables of choice (carrots, asparagus, tomato, etc.)	16 oz.
White cheddar & Feta cheese or cheese of choice	8 oz.

Method

Preheat the oven 425 F and line a tray with parchment paper.

Wash and cut all the vegetables into the desired shapes. The asparagus stalks should be peeled, and the very woody end of the asparagus should be removed. The carrots should be cut into thin slices. Next, grate the white cheddar cheese or cheese of choice. Set aside all the vegetables and cheeses.

Roll the galette dough until is about 1/8" thick and cut out 5" circles. You will get about 10/5" circles. Keep them cold until ready to use. Line up all the dough circles and top them with the cut- up carrots, asparagus, cherry tomatoes, and fresh basil or other herbs. Top with shredded cheddar cheese and crumbled feta over all the vegetables. Sprinkle with Celtic sea salt and olive oil to taste. Fold the edges of the dough as if you are wrapping the edges of a package and brush the dough of the galettes with the egg wash. Bake them for about 35 to 40 minutes until light golden brown and the bottoms of the galettes are fully baked. Serve immediately with a salad for lunch or a light dinner.

Baker's Tip:
You will get about 10/5" circles. Keep them cold until ready to use or freeze for up to two weeks with parchment paper in between the dough circles and then wrap them in plastic wrap. Take them out of the freezer the night before you intend to use the dough.

Pumpkin Mousse Tart or Pie

*GF, Paleo, Grain Free, RSF, DF Option**

Use this recipe to make a traditional American-style pumpkin pie or give it a more upscale look and feel with a European-style tart crust.

Pumpkin Tart or Pie

GF, Paleo, Grain Free, RSF, DF Option*

Makes a 1/10" tart. The tart crust can be made a day in advance and stored unbaked refrigerated until ready to use the next day. The pumpkin tart or pie is best eaten the same day as baked.

Dry ingredients		
1/10" almond coconut tart unbaked* pg. 82	1	
Pumpkin Puree	1 ½ Cups	12 oz.
Milk non-dairy	1 Cup	8 oz.
Celtic Salt	½ tsp.	
Cinnamon, Nutmeg ground	½ tsp.	
Cloves, ground	¼ tsp.	
Ginger, ground	¼ tsp.	
Eggs, Large	2	
Dates, pitted, whole	2	
Stevia, liquid	½ tsp.	
Chia gel binder	½ Cup	4.3 oz.

Method:

Prepare the tart shell and store it in the refrigerator until ready to bake. Preheat oven 350 °F.

Filling: In a food processor, mix the pumpkin puree, nondairy milk, salt, spices, eggs, chia gel binder, dates, and stevia. Pulse all the ingredients a few times until smooth and well blended. Set the filling off to the side and par-bake the unfilled almond coconut tart shell for about 15 to 20 minutes or until lightly golden brown, especially in the center of the tart. Once the tart is baked, fill it with the pumpkin filling and bake it for about 35 minutes or until the filling is set and the tip of a knife comes out clean. The texture of this tart is like a light custard or mousse. Allow the tart to cool completely and remove it from the tart pan. If you bake a pie, leave it in the pie dish. Serve with nondairy whipped cream or nondairy cream cheese icing. To make the cream cheese icing, just simply use vanilla and sugar of choice to taste and blend the ingredients until well blended and fluffy.

**Vegan options: replace ghee with nondairy butter in crust, see egg substitutions for pumpkin filling.*

Vanilla Apple Cobbler

*GF, DF, RSF, Paleo, *V Option*

Vanilla Apple Cobbler

GF, Paleo, Grain Free, RSF, DF Option*

This is a great fall and winter dish or dessert to go with your meals. I like to use firm, sweet, and tart apples like pink lady or Jonathan. These apples hold their shape beautifully, but, best of all, they contain loads of pectin. Pectin may help heal intestinal permeability, also known as leaky gut. See resources on this topic. The components of this dish can be prepared separately two to three days in advance. Just store the filling and streusel well covered in the refrigerator and assemble it the day needed. Serve warm.

Serves 9

Filling		
Apples, peeled, sliced, 2"x 3/8"	12 m	4 Lbs.
Arrowroot	3 tbsp.	
Water, room temperature	3 tbsp.	
Vanilla extract	1 tbsp.	
Ceylon cinnamon	½ tsp.	
Celtic salt	1 Pinch	
Stevia	¼ tsp.	
Myers Rum, optional	1 tsp.	
Streusel topping, see pg. 41	1 Batch	

Method:

You need one 9" x 9" x 2" square, glass, oven-safe, baking-safe dish. Preheat the oven to 350 °F.

Apple filling: wash, peel and slice all apples. Starting with 4 pounds, you will end up with about 3 pounds. Place the apples in a large, heavy- duty bottom pan and add cinnamon, salt, arrowroot, 3 tablespoon water, lemon juice. Cook covered until tender, but still holding the shape of the apple slices about 30 minutes on medium to slow heat. Stir the apples at least twice during the cooking process. Remove from heat when the apples are cooked, add stevia, vanilla and rum if desired, and set aside while the streusel is prepared. Transfer cooked apple mixture to baking dish, top with the streusel, and bake for about 35 minutes at 350 °F. The cobbler will be golden brown on top and the filling will be bubbly. Remove from the oven and allow it to come to room temperature. Can be eaten right away or stored in the refrigerator to be enjoyed over the next few days. Serve warm.

DF Option* use vegan butter or olive oil in streusel topping.

Streusel Topping

Streusel Topping

This streusel topping can be used for any sweet dessert tart or pie

Ingredients filling

Almond flour	1 Cup	3.5 oz.
Cassava flour	½ tbsp.	
Celtic Salt	1 Pinch	
Ghee or butter soft	2 tbsp.	
Olive oil	1tbsp.	
Vanilla extract	1 tbsp.	
Almonds whole, chopped optional	¼ Cup	

Method

In the food processor place the almond flour, cassava flour, pinch salt. Pulse few times until fully mixed. Next add the ghee or butter and pulse just twice until it resembles large to small crumb meal. Stop the food processor, add almonds, vanilla and stevia. Pulse just few times. Set off to the side until ready to use. Can be made the day before is needed if necessary. To use just crumble over the fruit of the pie or tart and bake as directed under the tart instructions.

Chapter Three

Breakfast Foods

Russian Tea Biscuits

Brioche Cinnamon Buns

Strawberry Shortcakes

Peach Scones or Strawberry Shortcakes

Blueberry Muffins

Banana Bread

Belgian Waffles

Raspberry Bakewell Coffee Cake

Creamy Buckwheat Quinoa Porridge

Eclairs

No Oatmeal Vanilla Chia Porridge

Baked Apples

Seasonal Fruit Bowl

Russian Tea Biscuits

Don't like poppy seeds? Use instead a raspberry or apricot jam filling. Egg wash the top with a light sprinkle of sugar. See resources for poppy seed filling.

Russian Tea Biscuits

Makes about 8 biscuits

Ingredients		
All-purpose flour	9 oz.	2 Cup, 2 tbsp.
Baking Powder	¼ oz.	2 ¼ tsp.
Sour cream	3 oz.	1/3 Cup, 1 tbsp.
Unsalted butter	6 oz.	¾ Cup
Whole large eggs	1	1
Egg yolk large	1	1
Orange zest optional	1 tsp.	1 tsp.
Filling		
Poppy seed filling*	1 Can	

Method:

In a small bowl, place the sour cream and eggs and mix well. In a second large bowl, measure and sift all the dry ingredients and mix well. Add the cold unsalted butter to the flour and use the rubbing method to incorporate the flour and butter together. The mixture will have a coarse meal texture. Add the sour cream and eggs mixture all at once and fold it into the flour mixture. You will have to finish bringing the dough together by hand. Gather the dough and flatten it into a disk. Wrap the dough in plastic wrap and let it rest in the refrigerator overnight.

The next day, take the dough out of the refrigerator, lightly dust a silicon mat, and roll the dough into a 9" x 14" rectangle. Spread a thin layer of raspberry jam over the roll dough. Sprinkle cinnamon, distributed chopped walnuts and golden raisins. Roll the dough into a cylinder away from you like a jelly roll. Make sure you roll the dough tightly. Cut the dough into strips1 ½ inches wide. Lightly whisk the leftover egg white and brush the top of the pastries with it. Sprinkle lightly with cinnamon and sugar to taste. Bake in a preheated oven 350 °F for about 25 to 30 minutes or until lightly golden brown. Cool in the pan for about 15 minutes and serve. Best the day they are baked, but the fully formed raw pastries can be frozen and baked at the last minutes straight from the freezer. Just follow the instructions given above to bake the biscuits.

> *Baker's Tip:*
>
> *A rubbing method is used to incorporate flour and butter together by rubbing them between your fingers. Cold butter should always be used for best results.*

*See Resources, p. 109

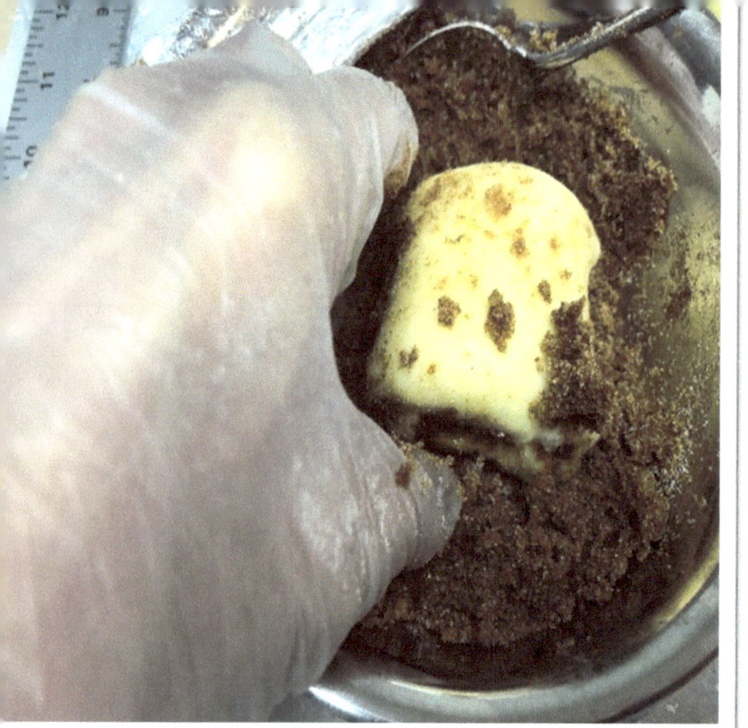

Brioche Cinnamon Buns

Brioche Cinnamon Buns

**RSF Option replace sugar with honey in dough.*

Brioche dough	541 g
Egg white for glue or water	1
Cinnamon	2 Tbsp.
Sugar	½ Cup
Brown butter icing pg.	

Method:

Preheat oven to 350°F.

Bake for about 20 to 25 min.
You will have to work quick to prevent the butter in the brioche dough from melting!
In a small bowl, mix the cinnamon and sugar. St aside this mixture; it will be used to coat the rolls on the outside just before baking and spread some of this mixture in the dough just before rolling the brioche dough and forming the cinnamon rolls.

Take the dough out of the refrigerator. Roll the Dough to flatten it to 1/8" thick, forming a 9" x 13" rectangle. Sprinkle the surface evenly the cinnamon sugar mixture, but stop sprinkling the sugar mixture 1" away from the wide edge furthest away from you and brush this edge with a bit of egg white. Working from left to right of the edge closest to you, tug the lip of the dough up and over the filling, keeping it tight. Roll up the dough tightening the log as you go. End with the edge facing down. Use a sharp knife or bench scraper to cut the rolls about 1-1/2 inches wide, about eight to nine rolls. Dip each roll into the remaining cinnamon sugar to coat the roll all the way around it. Place the cut-up rolls on the baking sheet lined with parchment paper and allow the rolls to rest covered at room temperature for 25minutes. Bake in a preheated oven 350 °F for about 20-25 minutes until golden brown. The sugar will caramelize around them. Wait about 10-15 minutes for the rolls to cool on the pan and then drizzle brown butter icing vanilla icing on them.

Baker's Tip:

For a reduced, refined, sugar-free version, use honey and cinnamon as a filler inside the cinnamon buns.

Strawberry Shortcakes

*GF, SF, Vegan, Paleo, Grain Free, SCD Option**

Peach Scones or Strawberry Shortcakes

*GF, DF, SF, Vegan, Paleo, Grain Free, SCD Option**

*This dough alternatively can be used to make strawberry or peach shortcakes simply by omitting the peaches in the dough. Instead slice the fresh peaches or strawberries and lightly sweeten them if necessary with your favorite sugar and spices. Top with nondairy whipped cream or, for a fun twist, use the honey common meringue recipe** and flambé just before serving! Use a biscuit cutter to give a traditional shape to the shortcake version.*

Ingredients		
Almond flour,	1.75 Cups	14 oz.
Baking soda	½ tsp.	
Baking powder, grain free, pg. 85	1 tbsp.	
Celtic salt	½ tsp.	
Wet ingredients		
Almond milk, unsweetened	½ Cup	
Stevia, liquid	½ tsp.	
Vanilla pure extract	1 tbsp.	
Avocado oil, cold process	¼ Cup	
Peaches, fresh, diced small	1 Cup	

Method:

Preheat oven to 350°F.

Bake for about 20 to 25 min.

In a medium bowl, measure and mix all the dry ingredients. In another bowl, whisk all the wet ingredients except the avocado oil. First add the oil to the dry ingredients and mix well with a fork. Next add all at once the wet ingredients into the dry ingredients mix until just combined; avoid overmixing. Next, fold in the diced peaches. Sprinkle extra almond flour over a large cutting board and place the dough over the almond flour. Sprinkle more almond flour on top of the dough and shape it into a square. Cut the square dough with a clean knife into eight triangles. Place the scones on a parchment lined tray. Bake in a convection oven for about 25 min, but rotate the pan halfway through the baking. The scones will be a light golden brown color once they are baked and slightly firm to the touch. Allow the scones to cool on the tray for a few hours. Serve the same day for best results. Once baked, I have kept them individually well wrapped in wax paper and stored in a plastic container for an extra three days. Serve with hot or iced tea or coffee!

**SCD option: omit the stevia and replace with honey.*

***Honey vanilla common meringue, p. 93, not vegan.*

Peach Scones

*GF, SF, Vegan Paleo, Grain Free, SCD Option**

Shape the almond dough with your hands into a square. The height of the dough is about 1 1/4" to 1 1/2". Avoid overworking the dough; dust the dough with extra flour on top and bottom to prevent the knife from sticking to the dough. Make sure the scones are spaced apart to ensure proper browning and baking. Bake immediately in a preheated oven.

Strawberry Shortcakes

Prepare the dough for the shortcakes the same way the peach scones were made, but omit the peaches. Cut the shortcake dough the same height as the scones, but use a round shape biscuit cutter to give the shortcakes their traditional shape.

Simply by omitting the fruit in the dough you can make the shortcakes!

Blueberry Muffins

Paleo, GF, DF, Grain Free, SCD, Nut Free

Blueberry Muffins (Fruit Muffins)

GF, DF, RFS, SCD, Paleo Friendly

Dry ingredients

Honey raw	¼ cup	2.5 oz.
Vanilla	1 tsp.	
Milk, coconut, or your choice	1 cup	8 oz.
Egg large each	2	
Olive oil	¼ cup	2 oz.
Blueberries fresh	1 cup	1 pint
Salt Celtic	1/2 tsp.	
Baking Soda	1 tsp.	
Baking Powder grain free, pg. 85	1 tsp.	
Gelatin plain	1 tsp.	
Coconut flour	1 Cup	3.3 oz.
Cinnamon optional		

Method:

Preheat oven to 400°F.

Bake for about 20 to 25 min.

In a medium bowl, measure and mix all the dry ingredients. In another bowl, whisk all the wet ingredients and eggs. Add all at once the wet ingredients into the dry ingredients until just combined; avoid overmixing. Next, fold in the blueberries. Use a scoop to distribute the batter into a muffin tin, lined with parchment paper cups, and sprinkle the tops with cinnamon. Bake in a convection oven for about 20–25 min, but rotate the pan halfway through the baking. Keep an eye during the last 10 min of baking to prevent over baking and drying the muffins. The bottoms of the muffins can get dark quickly.
For the sugar-free option, omit honey and replace with monk golden sweetener.

Baker's Tip:
The fruit muffins can be made with other combinations of fruits; just make sure they are juicy because the coconut flour will absorb all the moisture.

Banana Bread

*GF, DF, SCD, Paleo, Grain Free, RSF**

Banana Bread

GF, DF, SCD, RSF, Paleo, Grain Free

Dry ingredients

Honey raw*	2 tbsp.	
Vanilla	1 tbsp.	
Milk, coconut, or your choice	¼ Cup	
Egg large each	4	
Olive oil	¼ cup	2 oz.
Salt Celtic	1/2 tsp.	
Almond flour	2 Cups	200 g
Baking Soda	1 tsp.	
Baking Powder grain free pg. 85	1 tsp.	
Coconut flour	¼ Cup	
Cassava flour	2 tbsp.	
Cinnamon	1 tsp.	
Nutmeg	¼ tsp.	
Bananas very ripe	2 Cup	16 oz.

Method:

Preheat oven to 350°F.

Materials: Eight cavity mini loaf pans, lightly oiled with olive oil or a 9" x 5" loaf pan lined with parchment paper.

Bake for about 30 to 35 min.

In a medium bowl, weigh all the dry ingredients and mix well. Set aside. Next, mash the bananas in the food processor and add the remaining wet ingredients: coconut milk, vanilla, eggs, honey and olive oil. Pulse twice until well blended and emulsified. Next add the dry ingredient mixture all at once to the banana mixture and pulse just until combined.

Place the batter in a 9" x 5" pan that has been fully lined with parchment paper or use eight mini loaf pans greased lightly with olive oil. Bake for about 30 to 35 min until bread is set and golden brown. Allow the loaves or loaf to cool in the pan for about 10 min and then unmold and enjoy.

Baker's Tip:

The bananas must be very ripe to obtain the best flavor out of the bread.

Belgian Waffles

DF, RSF* Option*

Belgian Waffles

*DF & RSF Option**

This recipe was used by my mother-in-law to feed her large family. The recipe has been in the family for over 100 years, and I do not know where it came from because I never asked her, and now she has passed on. The waffles are delicious and light, but they take a bit of preparation.

Dry ingredients		
All-purpose unbleached flour	2 ½ cup	10 oz.
Celtic salt	½ tsp.	
Sugar*	1 tbsp.	
Active yeast	2 ¼ tsp.	1 pkg. 7 g
Milk, * warm	2 cups	
Unsalted butter*	½ cup	4 oz.
Pure vanilla extract	1 tbsp.	
Eggs, large, separated	4	

Method:

Sift the flour and salt and set aside. Proof the yeast by placing it into the warm milk (95 °F) and honey. Allow it to proof for at least 5 min. The yeast will become foamy and creamy if active.

Once you have determined it is active, whisk the egg yolks into the milk mixture one at a time until fully incorporated. Next add flour and vanilla extract all at once and whisk once again until fully incorporated.

In a clean 4 1/2 -quart mixer bowl, whisk all egg whites until they form soft peaks. Avoid over whipping the egg whites because this will cause the waffles to be dense and hard.

Once the egg whites have come to a soft peak, take about a ¼ portion of the egg whites and mix it into the batter until fully incorporated. Initially using a small amount of the egg whites will ensure that the remaining egg whites will provide sufficient air to lift the batter and make the waffles light.

Fold the remaining whipped egg whites into two portions. Cover the batter and allow it to rise and double in size. During the last 15 min, heat up your waffle iron. Proceed as per the instructions on your waffle maker. Serve warm with berries, maple syrup, or honey. Enjoy!

> *Baker's Tip:*
> *Fluffy waffles are produced by using whipped egg whites that are whipped to a soft stage and gently folded into the batter. *For option DF and RSF, replace the milk products with an alternative milk of choice and sugar for honey.*

Raspberry Bakewell Coffee Cake

GF, LF, SCD, Paleo, Grain Free, SF

Raspberry Bakewell Coffee Cake

GF, LF, Paleo, Grain Free, SF

Dry ingredients

Almond flour	2 cups	6.34 oz.
Cassava flour	1 tbsp.	9 g
Coconut flour	3 tbsp.	18 g
Baking powder, grain free, p. 85	1 tbsp.	
Celtic salt	1 pinch	
Eggs, large, separated	3	
Egg yolk, large	1	
Ghee, soft, not melted	½ cup	3.5 oz.
Pure vanilla extract	1 tbsp.	
Chia seed gel	½ cup	
Stevia liquid	½ tsp.	
Almonds whole, chopped fine	2 tbsp.	
Fresh raspberries	1 box	6.3 oz.
Raspberry jam, seedless. Your choice.	½ cup	

Method:

Preheat oven to 350 F. Prepare an 8" round cake pan with parchment paper, grease it with ghee, and coat it with almond flour.

In a food processor, mix well the almond flour, cassava flour, coconut flour, grain free baking powder, and a pinch of salt. Add the soft ghee and pulse once or twice until you have an evenly distributed ghee. The mixture will resemble a coarse meal texture. Next, add all at once the egg yolks, stevia, vanilla, and chia gel. Pulse once or twice just until barely mixed and loose. Set it off to the side, and, in a clean mixer bowl free of grease, whip the egg whites until they form a soft peak. Next take ¼ of the egg whites and mix it into the flour-butter mixture until evenly distributed. * Gently fold the rest of the egg whites and divide it into two portions until evenly distributed. Place half the batter into the prepared 8" pan and cover it with ½ cup seedless raspberry jam of choice and top with fresh raspberries. Reserve some fresh raspberries for the top of the coffee cake. Next add the remaining batter on top of the fresh raspberries and smooth with an offset spatula. Top the batter with saved fresh raspberries and chopped almonds. Bake in the middle of the oven for about 30 min until golden brown or, when tested, a toothpick comes out clean with one or two crumbs. Cool on a wire rack for about 10 min and, when cool, transfer it to a cake platter. Serve with extra fresh raspberries.

> *Baker's Tip:*
>
> *Fruit-sweetened jam is the best choice. *In this step, you sacrifice a small amount of eggs for the maximum aeration and egg distribution.*

Creamy Buckwheat Quinoa Porridge

GF, DF, SF, NF

This buckwheat quinoa porridge was served with a baked apple (see page p. 64).

Creamy Buckwheat Quinoa Porridge

GF, DF, SF, NF

I use Bob's Red Mill cracked groats "Creamy Hot Buckwheat Cereal."

Serves 2

Dry ingredients	
Cracked, creamy buckwheat groats	4 tbsp.
Quinoa, whole grain.	2 tbsp.
Water	1 cup
Celtic salt	1 pinch
Ceylon cinnamon	½ tsp.
Vanilla pure extract	1 tsp.
Almond milk, unsweetened	½ cup
Stevia to taste, liquid	2 drops

Method:

First wash the quinoa whole grain. In a small pot, place the creamy cracked buckwheat groats, washed quinoa, water, and a pinch of salt. Cook it until tender, about 10 min. After the first 10 min of cooking, add almond milk, Ceylon cinnamon, stevia, and vanilla and cook it for an additional 8–10 min or until creamy. Serve warm with fresh blueberries and roasted seeds like pumpkin or sunflower seeds. *Optional serve baked apple (p. 64) instead of the above suggestion. Top with presoaked chopped walnuts.

Baker's Tip:

Be patient when cooking this porridge. You may have to add more liquid, either water or almond milk, to acquire the desired creamy consistency.

Eclairs

You can make eclairs or puffs pastries with this recipe. All you have to do is decide the shape of the pastry. Round or elongated as seen in this photo. Filled with a creamy vanilla infused pastry cream, ice cream or mousse and fruit. You decide! This one is filled with vanilla infused pastry cream and glazed with Belgian chocolate ganache. Enjoy for breakfast with a cup of coffee or tea.

Dry ingredients	
10/5" Eclairs, baked, pg. 95	1 Batch
Vanilla Pastry Cream, pg. 91	1 Batch
Hard Ganache, 75°F temp.	1 Batch

Method:

Decide if you want to cut the éclairs in half to fill or use a long pastry tip shaped round at the opening to fill the eclairs or cream puffs from underneath the shell without cutting the shell in half.

If you have baked them the day before, it might be beneficial to re-bake in pre-heated oven for at least 10 minutes at 350 °F. The shells will be crispy and will last longer firm. In the photo, I chose to cut them in half, but have filled eclairs or cream puffs both ways. Use a pastry bag for either method to keep the process clean and simple. Once the shells are filled with the pastry cream, you are ready to ice with Belgian chocolate ganache. Dip each shell upside down half way into the ganache and shake lightly the excess ganache before reinverting the shell upright. Set the iced eclairs on a platter and store in refrigerator until ready to serve. Best eaten the same day.

No Oatmeal Vanilla Chia Porridge

GF, DF, SF, Grain Free, Paleo

Dry ingredients	
Chia gel	¼ cup
Celtic salt	1 pinch
Gala apple (large), grate fine, peeled	1
Ceylon cinnamon	½ tsp.
Vanilla pure extract	1 tsp.
Nondairy milk, unsweetened	¼ cup
Stevia to taste, liquid	2–3 drops

Method:

In a small pot, place the chia gel, a pinch of salt, almond milk, and finely grate the peeled apple. Cook until tender (about 10 min). Add Ceylon cinnamon, stevia, vanilla, and cook for an additional 5 min or until creamy and slightly thick. Serve warm with an extra sprinkle of cinnamon. Optional: Add a few tablespoons of water if you want porridge of thinner consistency.

> *Baker's Tip:*
>
> *Peel the apple and dice or grate the apple for a very creamy consistency. Leaving the skin behind will cause the hard peel to remain unbroken.*

Baked Apples

GF, DF, SF, Grain Free, Paleo

Apples are great for breakfast! They are nutrient dense and provide many benefi ts to the body (see p. 19 for more about the health benefits of apples, especially to the digestive system).

Serves 4

Dry ingredients

Gala apple, large	4
Ceylon cinnamon	1 tsp.
Water	2 tbsp.

Method:

Wash and cut the bottom of the apples and remove the top of the core of the apple, leaving a well in the center of each apple. In a small baking dish, place 3 tbsp. of water. Place the apples on top of the water in the baking dish and put 1 tsp. of water in the well of each apple and sprinkle a generous amount of Ceylon cinnamon. Bake in a preheated oven for about 20 min or until soft. When the apples cook to a soft or almost apple sauce texture, they release pectin. This pectin feeds the friendly bacteria in the colon and has the ability to heal a leaky gut. The pectin texture is like a light gel! Serve warm for breakfast or as a snack.

Optional: Serve with almond yogurt and homemade granola for another delicious breakfast idea. *SEE Paleo Granola,* p. 97

Seasonal Fruit Bowl

GF, DF, SF, Grain Free, Paleo

A seasonal fresh fruit bowl is a quick way to have breakfast in the morning. It is loaded with antioxidants that fight inflammation in the body, and it contains many vitamins and minerals. Vitamin C is usually found in large amounts in fruit. This vitamin is a key micronutrient in wound healing and the regeneration of collagen. Pair it with foods rich in zinc and you have a powerhouse for healing and producing collagen. This recipe can be doubled or quadrupled very easily to feed a crowd. Always use seasonal fruit and vegetables. If you have problems with spikes of blood sugar, add greens to your fruit bowl. The leafy greens will slow down the absorption of the natural sugar. The sugar found in fruits is not the same as added sugar due to the many micronutrients and macronutrients that aid in healing and maintaining a healthy digestive system and body overall.

Dry ingredients

Mango	¾ cup
Strawberries	¾ cup
Banana, medium	1
Blueberries	½ cup
Chia jam, p. 88	2 tbsp.

Method:

Wash and cut the fruit into bite sizes and place them in a small fruit bowl. Top with 2 tbsp. of chia jam or chia gel binder. Sprinkle cinnamon to taste.

Fresh Strawberries, mango, kale, and chia gel binder

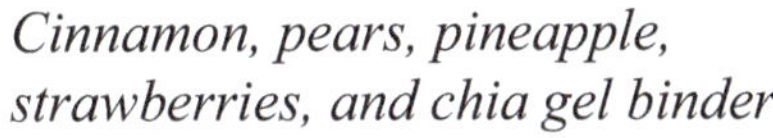

Cinnamon, pears, pineapple, strawberries, and chia gel binder

Chapter Four

Breads

Brioche Bread

*Sunflower Sourdough Bread**

Sourdough Culture or Levain

Artisan Multigrain Harvest Bread

*Seeded and Nutty Bread**

**Gluten free*

Brioche Bread

Brioche Bread

This dough makes light, delicious cinnamon rolls or French toast! The dough must be prepared the day before it is needed. The shelf life of the dough is two days.

Dry ingredients	
All-purpose flour	169.3 g
Bread flour	50.7 g
Salt	4.47 g
Sugar	26.8 g
Yeast, fresh	8 g
Wet ingredients	
Water, cold	21 g
Eggs, cold	118.6 g
Butter, 82% fat	110 g
Total weight	541.2 g

Method:

Mix the flours, salt, and sugar together very well into the bowl of a mixer. Set it aside and get the hook attachment ready. In another bowl, measure out the yeast, cold water, and eggs and mix them together to dissolve the yeast. Set aside. Measure out the butter and cut it into small cubes. Set it aside.

Place the bowl that holds the flour into the mixer and mix the dry ingredients once or twice with the hook attachment. Add all the wet ingredients all at once and mix them until they form a cohesive dough that pulls away from the bowl. After about 5 min of mixing, test a small piece of dough by stretching it. This is called the window test. If the dough forms a thin window that you can see through it without breaking, the dough is ready and strong. Next, add the cubed cold butter all at once and continue to mix it until it is well incorporated. This will take several minutes. Store the dough in the refrigerator overnight. Use the dough the following day to make a brioche loaf or my irresistible cinnamon brioche rolls (see p. 47). To shape into a loaf, you have two options: (1) Roll the dough out to the size of the loaf pan and fold it into thirds, like a brochure; (2) divide or weigh your dough into eight equal balls. Roll them gently on the table in a circular motion until uniform in shape, round, and smooth. Place all eight balls of dough into a parchment-lined loaf pan. Allow the dough to rise to double in size, about 30 min to one hour, depending on the temperature. Just before baking, brush with egg wash of egg whites and bake at 350 °F for about 30 min or until golden brown and set. Allow the bread to cool in the pan for at least 30 min before removing from the pan. Allow the bread to cool for at least two hours before cutting into slices.

Sunflower Sourdough Bread

GF, DF, RSF

The secret to a great-tasting artisan sunflower bread is to roast the seeds ahead of time before making the bread. Always use a scale when baking bread. The results will be consistent! To make this bread, the levain has to be prepared two days before baking. A baking stone is not required, but it produces a delicious and beautiful crust. Alternatively, to a baking stone you can use a cast iron skillet or Dutch Pot with lid during the baking process.

Sunflower Sourdough Bread

GF, DF, RSF

Dry ingredients		
French flour, blend 1, p. 92	200 g	7 oz.
Sunflowers, roasted, ground fine like flour seed	80 g	2.82 oz.
Psyllium husk	9 g	1 tbsp.
Sea salt	7 g	1.5 tsp.
Yeast, instant	8.2 g	2.25 tsp.
Sunflower seeds, whole roasted	30 g	4 tbsp.
Wet ingredients		
Water, temp 95–105 F	250 g	9 oz.
Yacón syrup	9 g	1 tbsp.
Levain, p. 72	120 g	4.2 oz.

Method:

Preheat oven and stone, 465 °F 20 minutes before baking bread. Five minutes before baking the bread, Place a small baking tray with ½ cup of water in the bottom of the oven. This will produce steam through the baking and prevent the bread from developing a crust before it has risen enough.

In a mixer bowl, 5-quart capacity, mix flours, seeds and salt together. Set aside and get the paddle attachment ready. In another bowl, measure out the yeast and the liquid ingredients and mix them well. Add the wet ingredients to the dry ingredients and mix for about 5 min. Add the levain and mix well. Take the dough out of the mixing bowl and knead by hand form a cohesive dough. Shape it into a round boule, place it over a tray lined with parchment paper, and allow it to rise covered for about two hours. After the dough has doubled in size, score the loaf in the center, forming a cross pattern (or score as desired). Transfer the bread in the parchment paper to the hot baking stone or cast iron skillet. Bake at 465 F for about 35 to 40 min or until golden brown. When tapped on the bottom, the loaf should sound hollow. Another way of telling whether the loaf is baked is that, when lightly pressed, you will hear a crackling sound. Remove from the oven and allow it to cool for at least two to three hours before cutting the bread. Why wait? Residual heat continues to bake the bread internally, the texture will improve too, and no gumminess will be detected. This is a great bread for sandwiches or toast!

Total weight of ingredients is 654 grams. Total hydration is 66.2 percent.

Tips: Avoid opening the door during the first 25 min of baking. Rotate the loaf during the last 5 min of baking. Always preheat your stone or cast iron skillet before baking the bread as it will give the bread dough an extra rise. If using a bread basket, lightly dust the inside of it with flour for an even coating and proof dough in the basket. Invert the dough just before baking over a parchment paper and score dough. Proceed as above.

Sourdough Levain (Culture)

GF, DF, NS

A sourdough is also known as a levain.

A levain is a fermented culture (sourdough) that adds depth to the flavor of the bread and nutritional richness. This bread is delicious, and people don't even know it is dairy and gluten free!

Dry ingredients		
Sorghum flour		4 oz.
Active yeast	2.5 g	
Water, filter, non-chlorinated		5.5 oz.

Method:

In a medium-size bowl, mix the flour, active yeast, and water together. Cover the bowl, with plastic wrap and leave it at room temperature to ferment. Ferment for 2 days before using the levain to make the bread. Proceed with the bread recipe. Scale the proper amount of levain to make the artisan sunflower bread. The levain's shelf life is two days. *

Note: please avoid using chlorinated water as it will kill the natural occurring bacteria and yeast in the culture. Most city tap water is chlorinated. To use city water, you must allow it to sit for at least 1 hour to allow the chlorine gas to evaporate.

*If you wish for a sourer profile in your bread, you will have to feed the culture daily for at least 7 days and stop feeding 1 day before baking the bread.

Daily Feeding of a room temperature culture: In a clean bowl, use 3.5 oz., of the initial culture or starter, 5.5 oz. filter water, and 4 oz. sorghum flour. Mix all the ingredients well, cover culture, and discard leftover culture. To use the culture for bread baking, stop feeding the culture for at least 24 hours, but it needs to be used within 2 days. The culture can be kept going by continual feeding resulting in a mild, sweet-sour aroma. If your culture does not smell right or changes in color significantly, discard and start again.

Artisan Multigrain Harvest Bread

Dry ingredients

French bread, mix-	4 cups	16 oz.
Celtic salt	1 tsp.	
Plain collagen, gelatin	2 tsp.	
Psyllium husk, powder, organic	1 tbsp.	9 g
Baking powder, grain free, p. 85	2 tbsp.	
Baking soda	1 tsp.	
Nigella sativa, ground	1 tsp.	
Whole cooked grain of choice**	½ cup	
Fruit or vegetable Puree of choice	½ cup	4 oz.
Olive oil*	¼ cup	
Apple cider vinegar	1 tbsp.	
Sparkling mineral water, plain	1 ½ cups	12 oz.

Method:

Preheat the oven to 425 F. Line a 9" x 5" loaf pan with parchment paper or free-form bread over parchment paper on a flat tray. No need to grease or flour the tray or loaf pan. Place a small pan in the oven with about ¼ cup of water. This water will eventually become steam, giving the opportunity for the bread to rise and expand before the crust is baked.

Mix all the dry ingredients into a 4 ½ quart mixer bowl. In another bowl, mix all the wet ingredients together. Add all at once all the wet ingredients to the dry ingredients. Mix for about 1–2 min by hand. Next, place the bowl in the mixer with the paddle attachment and mix for 1 ½ to 2 min until the batter becomes a cohesive dough that comes away from the bowl. Lightly knead the dough and shape it into a free-form batard or loaf shape. There's no need to do a traditional fold and shape with the dough. Place it into a 9" x 5" loaf pan or baking tray lined with parchment paper. Brush the top of the bread with extra olive oil and top with finely ground nigella sativa seeds, about ½ tsp. Score the bread ¼" deep. Place the bread dough in the preheated oven to bake for about 45 min or until the loaf sounds hollow, it's golden brown, or, when lightly pressed, it releases a light crackling sound. Rotate the bread during the last 5 min. Remove the bread from the pan as soon as it comes out of the oven and allow it to cool completely on a wire rack. To cut the bread, wait at least two to four hours. Otherwise, the bread texture will be gummy. The reason for this is that bread continues to cook as it cools down due to residual heat within the bread.

**For lower fat content, replace half of the olive oil with carbonated water.*

*** Grain of choice: cooked quinoa or cooked creamy buckwheat hot cereal from Bob's Red Mill*

Artisan Multigrain Harvest Bread

GF, DF, NO YEAST, Vegan, SF*

Apple-based bread gets a rustic brown rich color from the apples. Bake it in a loaf pan. Replace the pumpkin puree for apple sauce. I use a 4 oz. baby food jar organic.

Buckwheat Cracked Cereal Preparation Different Flavor Profile

Replace the cooked quinoa with the cooked cracked buckwheat groats.

Add ¼ cup of Bob's Red Mill creamy buckwheat hot cereal to ½ cup of boiling water. Let it sit for 5 min and cool completely before using to make the bread. Don't use the grains hot to make the bread because you will affect the texture of the bread. Feel free to try other grains.

The puree fruits and vegetables that I have tried are pumpkin, apple, pears, butternut squash, sweet potato, and others.

The baking powder is grain free, and I have provided the recipe in this book. Most commercial baking powders contain cornstarch, preservatives, and aluminum. It is worth making your own.

This bread has grains that are rich in many minerals and vitamins. It also contains pumpkin, which is what adds its golden color and richness; however, it does not taste like pumpkin.

Seeded and Nutty Bread

GF, DF, NO YEAST, Vegan, SF

Seeded and Nutty Bread

GF, DF, NO YEAST, Vegan, SF

Makes two small loaves

This bread is keto friendly because it is low in carbohydrates, but if you're watching your intake of fats, use caution as to how many slices you eat in a day. This bread is rich in healthy omega 3 and omega 6 fats from the nuts and seeds. I use Bob's Red Mill creamy buckwheat hot cereal to make this bread. Serve with wedges of aged cheese or jam. Delicious!

Dry ingredients		
Sunflower seeds, roasted	50 g	
Flax seeds	50 g	
Pumpkin seeds	50 g	1.7 oz.
Hemp seeds hearts	25 g	
Almond flour	100 g	
Buckwheat, creamy hot cereal***	165 g	
Water, filtered	328 g	12 oz.
Sea salt	2 tsp.	
Olive oil	78 g	
Chia gel binder	58 g	
Psyllium husk organic powder		2 tbsp.
Extra seeds, unroasted, for topping, optional		

Method:

Preheat oven to 400 F. Line two 2" x 6" loaf pans with parchment paper. No need to grease or flour the pans because the seeds and nuts are rich in oils and are what give this bread a shine and golden color. Scale and roast all the seeds at once. Avoid not roasting the seeds, especially the sunflower seeds, because the bread will have no flavor, and you will taste the raw sunflower seeds too. If you are pressed for time, you can omit grinding the nuts in a spice grinder, but be aware the crumb of the bread will be larger due to the seeds. Allow the seeds to cool first before grinding them and then proceed with grinding the seeds to a flour consistency. I like the texture that the ground seeds give the bread because it's reminiscent of an old-fashioned, dense, German bread like Vollkornbrot. Next, in a large bowl, place all the dry ingredients and mix well. In a microwave bowl, place the creamy cracked buckwheat cereal and half of the water (¾ cup) in the bowl and mix well. Cover the bowl lightly with a plate and microwave for about 2 min. Remove it from the microwave and allow it to rest covered for about 5 min. Once the 5 min are up, stir the buckwheat well and add to the dry ingredients along with the chia gel binder and olive oil and mix well by hand. Divide the dough into the two prepared pans and bake for about 55 min or until the bottom of the loaves sounds hollow, and they're golden brown.

Chapter Five

Culinary Basics

Pâte Sablée

Pâte Brisée

Almond Coconut Tart Dough

Vegan Tart Dough

Ghee

Grain-Free Baking Powder

Chia Gel Binder

Strawberry or Cherry Chia Jam

Cherry Banana Sorbet

Brown Butter Icing

Vanilla-Infused Pastry Cream

French Flour Bread Mix 2

Honey Vanilla Common Meringue

Pate Choux

Pâte Choux

Hard Ganache

Paleo Granola

Pâte Sablée

This is a tart dough with a soft, cookie-like texture. The dough must be made the day before it is needed. This is a delicious traditional French tart dough!

Ingredients

Unsalted butter	8 oz.	1 cup
Powdered sugar 10x	5 oz.	
Almond flour, blanched	5.5 oz.	
Egg, large, each	1	
All-purpose flour	10 oz.	
Vanilla extract		1 tbsp.

Method:

In a mixer bowl, cream the soft butter and sugar until it is very creamy, and add all the almond flour all at once, including the vanilla, and continue to beat until creamy. Add the egg and beat until fully incorporated. Stop the mixer. Fold in the flour, ⅓ at a time, until just blended. Avoid overmixing or your dough will become tough. Gather the dough, flatten it into a disk, and wrap it in plastic. Store it in the refrigerator overnight to be used the next day. The tart dough can be rolled a day in advance into tart molds or rings and later filled and baked, but it must be stored in the refrigerator. Extra dough can be frozen to be used at a later date. Bake at 350 °F for 12-15minutes or until golden brown or as instructed in recipes.

Pâte Brisée

Dough for savory or sweet galettes.

Dry ingredients		
All-purpose flour, non-bleached	3 cup	12 oz.
Cake flour, non-bleached	1 cup	4 oz.
Celtic salt	1 ½ tsp.	
Unsalted butter, cut into small cubes	1 cup	8 oz.
Water, iced	½–1 cup	
Egg yolks, large	2	

Method:

In a large bowl, mix the premeasured flours and salt until fully combined. Add the cut cubes of cold butter into the center of the flour and proceed with the rubbing method. The rubbing method is the process of rubbing the flour and butter together with your fingers until it resembles a coarse cornmeal. Next, whisk the egg yolks and about half the cold water together and add it all at once to the butter-flour mixture. Use a spatula to fold all the flour mixture and egg-water mixture together. The amount of additional water you will need to add to the dough will depend on the humidity and temperature of your work area. This is especially true when going from winter to summer. You can always add more water, but it will not be able to remove the excess of water without affecting the texture and flakiness of the dough. Once you have a cohesive dough, gather the dough into a flat disk and wrap it in plastic. Refrigerate it for a minimum of one hour or overnight for best results and the flakiest crust.

The next day, proceed by rolling the dough to the desired serving size and adding your favorite filling, whether sweet or savory. Bake free-form tarts at 400 °F for about 35 to 40 min or until golden brown and the bottom of the tarts are fully baked.

Baker's Tip:

Always work with very cold dough.

If you have excess dough, you can freeze it for up to two weeks. To use, place frozen dough in the refrigerator the day before you intend to use it.

Almond Coconut Tart Dough

*GF, LF, SF, SCD, Paleo, Grain Free, DF Option**

Makes a 1/10" tart that can be made a day in advance and stored unbaked until ready to use.

Dry ingredients		
Almond flour	2 cups + 2 tbsp.	7. oz.
Coconut flour	¼ cup	1.02 oz.
Cassava flour	1 tbsp.	
Baking powder, grain free p. 85	⅛ tsp.	
Celtic salt	1 pinch	
Pure vanilla	1 tbsp.	
Ghee*, soft room temperature	½ cup	3.45 oz.
Egg, large	1	

DF option replace ghee with a vegan butter.*

Method:

In a food processor, mix all the flours, baking powder, and salt. Pulse a few times until well mixed.

Next, add the ghee and pulse a few times until it resembles a coarse meal. In a small bowl, whisk the egg lightly with the vanilla and add it all at once to the butter-flour mixture. Pulse a few more times until the dough comes together into a light mass. Do not overmix.

This dough is very easy to handle and use immediately in a tart pan. Spread the dough until evenly distributed on the sides and bottom of the tart pan. Place a piece of parchment paper, and cut to the size of the tart shell, over the tart. Next, use the flat bottom of a measuring cup to smooth the dough, pressing the dough lightly until it is evenly distributed and thin enough to be cut with a fork once the tart is shaped and baked. Dock the dough lightly with a fork, but avoid piercing holes straight through the dough because this will cause the fillings to leak out of the tart shell during the baking process. Let it rest in the refrigerator for about 5–10 min before baking. Bake at 350 °F for 15–18 min or until golden brown. This tart dough is perfect for many sweet or savory tarts.

Vegan Tart Dough

GF, SF, Vegan

Makes a 1/10" tart. It can be made a day in advance and stored unbaked until ready to use. This dough has a crunchy, cookie-like texture, and it can be made into crackers, flavored with all sorts of herbs, spices, and sea salt.

Dry ingredients

Almond flour	2 cups + 2 tbsp.	7. oz.
Coconut flour	¼ cup	1.02 oz.
Cassava flour	1 tbsp.	
Baking powder, grain free, p. 85	⅛ tsp.	
Celtic salt	1 pinch	
Pure vanilla	1 tbsp.	
Vegan butter, soft or room temp.	½ cup	3.45 oz.
Chia egg replacement, p. 87	¼ cup	

Method:

In a food processor, mix all the flours, baking powder, and salt. Pulse a few times until well mixed. Add the vegan butter and pulse a few more times or until it resembles loose cornmeal. Next, add the vanilla and chia gel egg and pulse one more time until the dough comes together.

Select a 10" ring pan or tart pan, set over a baking tray lined with parchment paper, and place the dough all at once into the tart pan. Next, use an offset spatula to slowly spread the dough all over the sides and bottom of the pan. Take a piece of parchment paper big enough to cover the top of the tart pan and cover the tart. Next, use a flat bottom measurement cup and use this cup to smooth the dough in the bottom of the tart pan. Apply gentle pressure on the parchment paper against the dough to smooth the edge of the dough. Allow the dough to chill in the refrigerator for 10 to 15 min before baking. Bake at 350°F for 15-20 minutes or until golden brown.

Ghee

GF, LF, SCD, Paleo

Ghee is a clarified butter made from cow's milk and is lactose free. During the process of making ghee, the milk solids are removed, making it friendly to people with sensitivities to dairy. It has a slightly higher concentration of fat and calories. The ratio of butter to ghee is about 1: ¾. The recipe below will yield about 1½ cups. Ghee originated in India.

Ingredients

Unsalted butter	16 oz.	2 cups

Method:

In a small sauce pan pot, place the unsalted butter and cook it over low heat until the mixture starts to bubble and turn slightly golden brown. This process will take at least 20–30 minutes, so be patient. Eventually you will see the milk solids separating away from the fat and sinking to the bottom of the pot. The ghee is ready when it has a light amber color and is very aromatic. The final product is delicious, and it has a nutty aroma. Set aside to cool slightly and strain through a fine strainer. When completely cool, store it in a glass jar and refrigerate until needed.

Grain-Free Baking Powder

GF, DF, V, Paleo, Grain Free

Making your own grain-free baking powder is easy. This recipe is grain free, and I came across it on the back of a Bob's Red Mill product. I love this company.

The original recipe makes too much. Here is just a fraction of it.

Ingredients

Baking Soda	1 tbsp.
Cream of Tartar	2 tbsp.
Arrowroot	2 tbsp.

Method:

In a small glass bottle with a wide mouth opening, place all the dry ingredients and mix well. Place the lid over the bottle and shake it well a few times. Label and store it in a cool, dry place in the pantry until ready to use. The product will last several months. Note if your ingredients are lumpy, it is best to sift the ingredients and then proceed per the above instructions.

Chia Gel Binder

GF, V, Paleo, Grain Free

Chia seeds are rich in omega 3 fatty acids, calcium, fiber, and iron. Chia seeds are versatile in that they are not only nutritious but also can replace eggs for vegan baking and can help make a dessert sugar free. They make a quick breakfast too! Always buy the chia seeds whole and grind them just before using them. Store in refrigerator to prevent staling and oxidation.

Ingredients

Chia seeds, ground	1/4 cup
Filtered water	1,1/4cups

Method:

In a small glass bowl, put the chia seeds and top with room temperature water. Stir once or twice to submerge the seeds in water. Cover the bowl with plastic wrap and store it in the refrigerator overnight until ready to use. Its shelf life is seven days. This binding gel is nutritious and can be added to make a full breakfast bowl with fresh fruit, alternative milk, hemp hearts, nuts, or hemp protein.

Chia gel binder can be used to replace sugar cup by cup, but to this you must add drops of liquid stevia to taste. In addition, see other sugar replacement choices, p. 17.

Chia Egg

Ingredients

Chia seeds	1 tbsp.
Filtered water	3 tbsp.

Method:

First grind the chia seeds in a spice grinder until they have a fine flour texture. In a small glass bowl, mix the ground chia seeds and water together. Stir until well blended. Use egg, as directed by the recipe. One large egg equals ¼ cup in volume.

Other Egg Replacement

1. Fruit can be used to replace eggs. Use ¼ of fruit puree, plus 1 tsp. of baking powder per large egg.
2. Flax seeds can be used to replace eggs. Use 1 tbsp. of pre-ground flax seeds to 3 tbs. of hot water. Let rest for about 3-5 minutes before using. Makes 1 large egg.
3. Gelatin Egg can be used to replace eggs. Source bovine. In a small container use 1 tbsp. of plain gelatin to 3 tbsp. of cold water. Mix well and allow it to bloom for 5 min., dissolved over a hot water pan until gelatin is clear and fluid. Use right away. Makes the equivalent replacement of 1 large egg.

Strawberry or Cherry Chia Jam

GF, V, Paleo, Grain Free

*Chia seeds are a versatile food that allows an otherwise sugar laden jam to be made sugarless. Just make sure you use in-season fruits because they are nutrient dense, aromatic, and very sweet when in season. *Replace with fresh cherries for cherry jam.*

Ingredients

Ingredients		
Strawberries* fresh, diced	2 cups	15 oz.
Lemon juice, fresh	1 tbsp.	
Chia gel binder, p. 86	¼ cup	2.1 oz.
Stevia, to taste	½ tsp.	
Celtic salt	1 pinch	

Method:

In a small pan, place the washed, diced strawberries, lemon juice, a pinch of salt, and the chia gel binder. Cook on medium to low heat until the fruit has sweat and comes to a boil. You may need to stir the jam a few times to prevent sticking or scorching. Once it comes to a boil, turn the heat off, but leave the jam on the stove, covered, and allow it to cook for an extra 2 min. Remove it from the stove and add ½ tsp. of stevia. Stir well and place it in clean glass jars. Store it in the refrigerator or, for a longer shelf life, freeze the jam in freezable containers. Note: for a thicker consistency jam, cook it longer at low heat to evaporate the liquid until the desired consistency is reached.

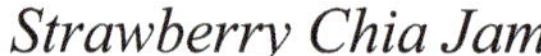

Strawberry Chia Jam

Cherry Banana Sorbet

GF, V, Paleo, Grain Free, SF

Easy to make. Just store frozen in-season sweet fruits and let your imagination run wild. It's easy to double or quadruple this recipe. You will just need to adjust water or almond milk to achieve the desired texture. Serves 1

Ingredients	
Banana ripe, frozen, large	1
Dark sweet cherries	⅓ cup
Water or unsweetened almond milk	1 tbsp.
Vanilla extract	½ tsp.

Method:

In a small food processor, place one frozen ripe banana, ⅓ cup of sweet frozen cherries, and water or almond milk and vanilla. Pulse until it has a fi ne texture that resembles a sorbet. It is best enjoyed right away, but it can be stored in the freezer. The texture will change a bit. Other variations are banana, vanilla, and chocolate chips; strawberry banana; or banana, Dutch cocoa powder, vanilla, almond unsweetened milk, and chocolate chips.

Don't be afraid of fruits spiking your blood sugar. Problems only arise when people mix fatty foods with fruits and then are not physically active.

Brown Butter Icing

GF, V, Paleo, Grain Free

This icing is delicious over any pastries like cinnamon rolls or coffee cakes.

Method:

Ingredients		
Heavy cream	½ Cup	4 oz.
Powder sugar, 6x or 10 x	1 cup	
Ghee or brown butter	1 tbsp.	
Pure vanilla extract	2 tsp.	

In a small bowl, place the powder sugar, vanilla, and heavy cream and mix well until fully dissolved. Add the ghee and mix well until smooth. Use immediately over your morning pastries or cinnamon buns. Any leftover icing can be stored in the refrigerator, covered and reheated just before using it again.

Vanilla-Infused Pastry Cream

GF, Grain Free, Option LF, RSF*

This vanilla-infused pastry cream can be used to fill cakes, pastries, or individual desserts, and variations can be accomplished easily and quickly by adding ingredients like orange peels, cinnamon, or more exotic flavors. Let your imagination be your guide. If you are not able to use cornstarch, replace it with potato starch.

LF option: Use lactose-free milk and lactose-free butter or ghee.*

Ingredients

Milk	2 cups	16 oz.
Egg yolks, large	4	
Honey	¼ cup	2 oz.
Pure vanilla extract	1 tbsp.	
Cornstarch	1 tbsp.	1.1 oz.
Butter, unsalted*	2 tbsp.	1 oz.

Method:

In a medium bowl, place the sugar, cornstarch, and half of the milk and whisk until fully dissolved. Add the egg yolks one at a time, whisking until fully emulsified into the sugar and cornstarch milk mixture. Set it off to the side. In a medium-size pot, place the other half of the milk and bring it to a full boil. Temper a small portion of the hot milk mixture into the sugar and egg yolk mixture and whisk quickly to prevent the eggs from curdling. Add the rest of the milk a bit at a time until fully incorporated. Return the milk mixture back to the heat and cook it until it boils. Allow it to boil no more than 1 to 2 min to cook the cornstarch taste off. Remove it from the heat. Immediately add the vanilla extract and unsalted butter to the custard. Stir it until fully dissolved and strain it immediately to remove any egg curds. Transfer it to a clean glass bowl and cover the custard with a piece of parchment paper and store it in the refrigerator until ready to use. The custard can be prepared one to two days ahead. Keep it refrigerated.

French Flour Bread Mix 2 (Hardier Flour Mix for Breads)

GF, V

Multigrain flour mix, loaded with many nutritious minerals that support health. You can replace half of the sorghum flour for millet flour for a different flavor profile. The Artisan Multigrain Harvest Bread was made by replacing half of the sorghum flour with millet flour.

Ingredients	
Arrowroot	544 g
Sorghum flour	653 g
Cassava flour	136 g
Organic ground, psyllium husk, powder	27 g

Method:

In a medium bin with a lid, weigh and mix well all the flours and psyllium husk. Store it in a dry container away from the light and heat to prevent oxidation and degradation of the nutritional content. Alternatively, you can use a mixer to blend all the flour and proceed as above to store the flours.

Honey Vanilla Common Meringue

GF, DF, RSF

A meringue is a light topping used to top cakes, desserts, pies, tarts, and much more. Your imagination is the limit. A perfect meringue will hold its shape and not become water logged the next day!

Ingredients

Egg whites, pasteurized		3 oz.
Honey, raw		4 oz.
Cream of tartar	⅛ tsp.	
Vanilla extract	½ tsp.	

Method:

Use a clean mixer bowl, rub a half- cut lemon in the inside of the bowl, and use the whisk attachment. Place the pasteurized egg whites inside the bowl and attach the whisk. Whisk the egg whites and cream of tartar at a high speed until frothy. Gradually add the honey and continue to whip until it forms stiff peaks that hold their shape. It may take up to 5 to 6 min to whip to a stiff peak and incorporate the honey. Use it immediately to ice your cake or pies. Note: Make sure to use the lemon to clean the bowl and whisk attachment before embarking on making the meringue. Any traces of grease will deflate your icing!

Pasteurized eggs are safe to eat raw. Use this meringue to top the pumpkin tart or lemon curd tarts for another dairy-free option.

Pate Choux

Medium consistency for piping pate choux is desired.

Eclairs Shape *Cream Puffs Shape*

Pâte à Choux

This is a versatile dough that is soft enough to pipe into many shapes, the most common being the éclair and cream puff. To ensure a successful shape and texture, you must bake them at high heat until the pate choux are dry and firm to the touch. Using all water in the Pâte à Choux produces a crispier pastry.

Ingredients

All-Purpose flour		6 oz.
Salt	Pinch	
Eggs		4 oz.
Unsalted butter	½ cup	4 oz.
Whole milk or water		8 oz.

Method:

In a small pot, bring to a boil the liquids and add a pinch of salt and butter. As soon as it boils, add the flour all at once and stir until the mixture comes together into a sticky dough. Cook for 1 or 2 more minutes to evaporate the liquids. Transfer the dough to a mixer bowl and attach the paddle to the mixer. Mix at medium speed for a few minutes to cool the dough slightly. Next add the eggs one at a time until mixed well. The dough will become slightly stiff, stiff enough to pipe. Bake Pâte à Choux at 425 °F for about 25 minutes or until golden brown and firm. Do not open the oven as it will cause eclairs to deflate.

Next get a disposable 12" piping bag and place a 1/2" round piping tip. Fill the bag halfway and pipe 5" logs on a baking tray lined with parchment paper. Tip to get uniform logs of pate choux: Mark your parchment paper with a pencil and reverse it when you're ready to pipe the éclairs.

Hard Ganache

GF, Grain Free

Ganache can be used to ice cakes, cookies, desserts, and top éclairs like the one that appears in the breakfast section of this book.

Ingredients

Heavy cream	1 cup	8 oz.
Belgian chocolate coins, semisweet or dark		8 oz.
Extract or spirit of choice, optional	1 tbsp.	

Hard ganache is pourable at 76 °F degrees.

Method:

Place the chocolate pieces or coins in a large mixing bowl. Gently boil the heavy cream in a heavy sauce pan at slow to medium heat. Bring the cream to a scalding point, where it will foam almost to the top of the bowl, but avoid scorching or letting the heavy cream boil over. Pour the hot cream over the chocolate coins and stir from the center of the bowl to the outer edges until the mixture is completely emulsified. Add liqueur or extract flavor of choice. Be certain the mixture is well blended to avoid grey streaks in the final results. Use it to ice your cake or pastries. The ideal temperature for the ganache for icing cakes or pastries is 75 °F.

Paleo Granola

GF, DF, RSF

I like to presoak and roast lightly my nuts and store them in the freezer for later use. In this recipe, the walnuts were the only nuts presoaked. Serve as a snack or for breakfast pair with a baked apple.

Ingredients

Pecan, whole	3 cups	12 oz.
Walnuts, halved	1 cup	3 oz.
Sunflower seeds, raw	½ cup	2.8 oz.
Coconut, shredded, unsweetened	½ Cup	1.5 oz.
Dates, presoaked, drained, diced	½ cup	
Celtic salt	½ tsp.	
Vanilla extract	1 tbsp.	
Cinnamon Ceylon	½ tsp.	
Yacón root syrup, p. 109	1 tbsp.	
Eggs	2 Large	

Method

In a medium bowl, place all the dry ingredients and yacón syrup. Mix ingredients until well blended. Next whipped two whole large eggs in a mixer until foamy about 1.5 minutes and add to the dry mixture all at once. Toss all the ingredients together until fully incorporated. Please note: you need to stir the granola around at least 2-3 times during the baking to ensure the granola is evenly toasted.

Bake in a preheated oven at 325°F for 20-25 minutes until golden brown or lightly roasted. Cool granola in the tray over a cooling rack. Once cool, store in a glass jar. Shelf life is about 7 days.

Photo below shows granola baked clusters.

Chapter Six

Nutritional Information on Gluten-Free Flours, Starches, and Others

Purple Gut Juice

Golden Milk Latte

Golden Milk Latte

Gallbladder Lemonade

Bright Red Blood Mover and Purifier Juice

Chai Tea, Hot or Iced

Black Raspberry Lemonade (Iced)

Oregano Tea for Infections

Resources

References

Glossary

Nutritional Information on Gluten-Free Flours, Starches, and Others

Flour Name	Protein	Fiber	Minerals	Vitamins	Antioxidants
Banana Flour Plantain	yes	yes	yes	yes	A
Brown Rice Flour	CQ	yes	yes	yes	A
Buckwheat Flour	CQ	yes	yes	yes	A
Chestnut Flour	yes	yes	yes	yes	A
Coconut Flour	yes	yes	yes	yes	A
Corn Flour	yes	yes	yes	yes	A
Fava Flour	yes	yes	yes	0	A
Garbanzo/Chick Pea Flour	yes	yes	yes	yes	A
Millet Flour	yes	yes	yes	yes	A
Oat Flour	yes	yes	yes	yes	A
Quinoa Flour	C	yes	yes	yes	A
Sorghum flour	yes	yes	yes	yes	A
Sweet Potato Flour	yes	yes	yes		A
Sweet Rice Flour	yes	0	0	0	A
Soy	CQ	yes	yes	yes	A
Teff	CQ	yes	yes	0	A
Tigernut	yes	yes	yes	yes	A
White Rice Flour	yes	yes	yes	yes	A
Arrowroot	yes	0	yes	yes	A
Cassava	yes	yes	yes	yes	A
Potato Starch	0	0	0	0	A
Tapioca	0	0	0	0	X

CQ = quality protein, missing lysine

Yes = medium traces of protein

0 = no Protein A

= antioxidants

X = no Antioxidants

Contain or are starches

C = complete protein

More nutritional analysis can be found here: https://ndb.nal.usda.gov/ndb/search/list

Purple Gut Juice

GF, DF, SF, Paleo

This juice has ingredients that many countries have used for centuries to heal intestinal issues. It can be used two to three times per week for about 30 days to repair the digestive system. Always use caution when implementing a new protocol in your healing journey.

Serves 1 (approximately 10 oz.)

Ingredients	
Celery sticks	2
Cucumber, large, peeled	1
Purple cabbage wedge	¼ head

Method:

Wash all the vegetables and peel the cucumber. Juice it per your juicer instructions. Serve it immediately to prevent oxidation and obtain the most nutritional benefits.

Golden Milk Latte

GF, DF, SF

The golden milk latte has many health benefits due to its blend of spices. It's also a delicious alternative to coffee for a hot morning drink!

Serves 1

I provide the recipe but also a small summary of the list of health benefits from the spices, p. 20.

Golden Milk Latte

GF, DF, SF

Personally, I prefer this latte made with cardamom rather than ginger, but ginger is more traditional in Ayurveda healing.

Ingredients

Almond milk, unsweetened	1 cup	8 oz.
Turmeric, ground	½ tsp.	
Ceylon cinnamon, ground	½ tsp.	
Ginger or cardamom, ground	⅛ tsp.	
Paleo protein, optional	1 tbsp.	
Stevia liquid	2–3 drop	

Method:

In a small pot, place all the ingredients, including almond milk. Cook on low to medium heat until it comes to a frothy stage, full boil. Watch because it will boil over very quickly. Serve it immediately and top with a slight sprinkle of extra Ceylon cinnamon.

If you decide to use the protein, add it to your cup and stir the hot milk into it. Do not boil the protein mix; the nutrients are sensitive to heat.

Gallbladder Lemonade

GF, DF, SF, Paleo

You're going to love this lemonade if you've not been able to enjoy lemonade in the summer because of the added sugar. This lemonade is refreshing, loaded with antioxidants, alkalizing properties, and it has malic acid from the apples, which may help dissolve gallbladder stones. Avoid using juices if you have small intestinal bacterial overgrowth. Serve over ice in the summer. Delicious!

Serves 2

Ingredients	
Celery sticks	2
Cucumber, large	2
Granny Smith apples, cored and quartered.	4
Lemon, peeled, no seeds.	½ or 1

Method:

Wash all the vegetables. Peel the cucumber and ½ lemon. Follow your juicer instructions to finish. Serve it immediately to prevent oxidation and obtain the most nutritional benefits. Great over ice!

Red Blood Mover and Purifier Juice

GF, DF, SF, Paleo, Vegan

This juice has ingredients that have many healing properties for the whole body and the ability to help cleanse or detox the liver and gallbladder. It also may help flush gallbladder stones.

Ingredients	
Celery sticks	2
Cucumber, large, peeled	2
Beet raw, peeled, med.	1
Kale leaves	2
Dandelion leaves	½ Cup
Lemon, peel	1/2
Arugula leaves	1Cup

Method:

Wash all the vegetables and peel the cucumber, lemon and beet. Juice per your juicer instructions. Serve immediately to prevent oxidation and obtain the most nutritional benefits.

Chai Tea, Hot or Iced

GF, DF, SF, Paleo

This tea is also a great warming tea with healing capabilities. Serve it for breakfast or afternoon tea, warm. Black tea contains tannic acid which is astringent, antibacterial and anti-enzymatic. Dentist have given the advice to patients for years after dental extractions to use a moist tea bag and light pressure after 20 hours to stop bleeding if necessary.

Ingredients	
Ginger, fresh, 1" piece	1"
Lemon grass, fresh, 2"	2
Black tea organic, 1 bag	1
Milk of choice, almond or dairy, splash, warm	1
Water, filter	2 Cups

Method:

Boil the water and wash the ginger and lemon grass. Place it on the bottom of the teapot, along with the bag of organic tea. Pour the boiling water (210 °F) over the tea, lemongrass, and ginger. Cover the teapot and steep for about 5 to 8 min. Serve it with a splash of warm milk of your choice. Enjoy it immediately or you can cool the drink down in the refrigerator to be enjoyed later and then served over ice.

Black Raspberry Lemonade (Iced)

If you are lucky enough to have access to fresh black raspberries, you can harvest some extraordinary health benefits. Medical research has shown black raspberries to be beneficial in the fight against oral cancer (see 8, p. 110*). Black raspberry extract can be used for many things, like ice cream, desserts, or smoothies. Use your imagination.*

GF, DF, SF, Paleo

Serves 2

Ingredients	
Fresh lemon, medium size	1
*Black raspberries, extract, pg.109	2 tsp.
Sparkling water	7-8 oz.
Stevia liquid, optional	2 drop

Method:

Wash the lemon and squeeze the juice. Mix it well with filtered sparkling water and the black raspberry extract and sweeten it to taste with stevia. Serve it over ice. It tastes so good and it's great for a hot summer day, and in the winter, you can enjoy it hot.

Don't worry, I've provided a good source to buy black raspberries (Note I have no monetary gain from this company; see resources, p. 109).

Oregano Tea for Infections

GF, DF, SF, Paleo

This herb has antioxidants that give it strong antibacterial, antiviral, and antifungal properties. It may be strong enough to get rid of gut or bladder infections. A perennial herb from the mint flowering family, known as brightness of the mountain, the chemical makeup that gives this herb its unique smell includes thymol, pinene, carvacrol, limonene, and others. When oregano is harvested into essential oil (7, p. 110), it produces strong and stable effects that may help fight off stubborn infections. It should not be used more than 14 days because it can cause a gut imbalance due to the strong antibacterial and fungal effect. When using essential oils, follow the manufacturer's instructions or your health-care provider's guidelines.

Ingredients	
Oregano, dry leaves	1 Tsp.
Water, filtered	6 oz.

Method:

Boil the water and place the washed oregano leaves in a tea bag. Steep the oregano tea for about 5 min. Drink three times per day for 7 to 14 days only.

Resources

Bob's Red Mill

5000 SE International Way, Milwaukie, OR 97222

Flours, starches, gluten-, and grain-free flours, seeds, yeast, nuts, and much more. It's also a fun place. You can tour the mill and store in Milwaukie, Oregon.

Online purchase is available too.

Manitoba Harvest

They sell hemp products, including protein hemp powders. Available online and through

Amazon. https://manitobaharvest.com/products/

Artichoke Store

Curated cookware collection. They sell tart pans, ring molds, scales and hard to find culinary bake or cookware. Visit online or the store in Cincinnati, Ohio 45202

https://www.artichokeotr.com/

Wassertrom Restaurant Equipment

Restaurant equipment supply store for bread pans and much more. Check your state for local shop locations.

Local Grocery Stores and Farmers Markets

Locally grown in-season fruits, organic and non-GMO vegetables, pasteurized egg whites, pasteurized raised organic eggs, herbs, and more.

BerriHealth

A good source for all black raspberry products. This is where I buy the black raspberry extract for the black raspberry lemonade recipe. It contains no alcohol. This is a reputable source for 100% black raspberries products.

https://www.berrihealth.com/collections/all/products/black-raspberry-extract

Solo Foods

Pastry fillings, I use the poppy seed filling in this book for the Russian tea

biscuits. Website: Solofoods.com

Alovitox.com

Certified Organic Yacón Syrup

References:

1. A. Chelating Agent. U.S. patent number 3160632 A, filed: January 30, 1961; awarded: December 8, 1964. Inventors: Toy Arthur Dock Fon, Eugene H Uhing; Stauffer Chemical Co.

2. B. Herbicide. U.S. patent number 3455675 A, filed: June 25, 1968; awarded: July 15, 1969. Inventors: Riyad Rida Irani, Mondanto Co.

3. C. Anti-microbial. U.S. patent number 20040077608 A1, filed: August 29, 2003; awarded: April 22, 2004. Inventors: William Abraham, Monsanto Technology Lic. Title: Glyphosate Formulations and Their Use for the Inhibition of 5-Enolpyruvylshikimate-3-Phosphate Synthase.

4. D. Biocide. U.S. patent number 7771736 B2 filed: August 29, 2003; awarded: August 10, 2010. A biocide is defined as any chemical substance or microorganism intended to destroy, deter, render harmless, or exert a controlling effect on any harmful organism. Inventor:(William Abraham)

5. Flour bleaching agents are food additives added to flour to make it appear whiter. They are not allowed in European countries (chlorine, bromate, peroxides),
   a. https://bakerpedia.com/processes/flour-bleaching/
   b. https://www.accessdata.fda.gov/scripts/cdrh/cfdocs/cfcfr/CFRSearch.cfm?fr=137.105
   c. https://www.organics.org/bleached-vs-unbleached-flour/

6. Effectiveness of Stevia Rebaudiana Whole Leaf Extract against the Various Morphological Forms of Borrelia Burgdorferi in Vitro. A.
   a. https://www.ncbi.nlm.nih.gov/pmc/articles/PMC4681354/

7. Oregano oil, medical research for E. coli and pseudomonas bacterial infections:

   https://www.ncbi.nlm.nih.gov/pubmed/23484421. Antiviral efficacy of oregano oil against the norovirus: https://www.ncbi.nlm.nih.gov/pubmed/24779581

8. Black raspberry extract and fractions contain angiogenesis inhibitors:
   a. https://www.ncbi.nlm.nih.gov/pubmed/15884816
   b. https://www.ncbi.nlm.nih.gov/pubmed/27594930

9. Conjugated linoleic acid in humans:
   a. https://academic.oup.com/jn/article/133/10/3041/4687585
   b. https://academic.oup.com/ajcn/article/85/5/1203/4632999

10. Melatonin:
    a. https://www.ncbi.nlm.nih.gov/pmc/articles/PMC3850896/

11. Hossain, Aftab & Saifullah, Md. (2019). The Effects of Nigella Sativa on the Immune Disorders.

Glossary

Terms as it relates to baking field.

1. **Bloom:** Gelatin needs to be softened in water before heating to melt. Soak the gelatin for 5–10 minutes to soften before heating. Gelatin can be bloomed in just about any liquid.

2. **Knead:** Kneading refers to the technique of making a bread dough cohesive and smooth prior to proofing and baking. Here is how: bring the dough out of the mixer bowl and on to the counter. Use the heal of your hand to push the dough out and away from you and then fold the dough on itself and repeat the motion again using the heal of your hand and fingers to gently bring the dough around. A wheat based bread that is done by hand may require 10–12 minutes of kneading to develop the gluten and with an electric mixer it might just be 5 minutes. Gluten free breads will only take 1–2 minutes of kneading to make the dough cohesive and smooth as the breads do not have gluten. Some laminated wheat-based doughs, such as brioche or croissant, require much more kneading.

3. **Temper:** Ln this book, tempering refers to bringing cold, or room temperature eggs, to the temperature of the hot liquid to prevent separation or curling of the eggs. Here is the technique: first whisk your eggs to separate them and break protein and fats; next take a small amount of the hot liquid and whisk quickly into eggs, adding slowly the hot liquid until you have added at least half of the hot liquid to eggs. Last, slowly add the remaining of the hot liquid to the egg mixture. Now you are ready to return the custard to the heat to finish cooking it. Tempering is also used in chocolate molding and production of chocolate with the same principal of heating and cooling. It helps prevent graying streaks, lumpy and separation of cocoa fat. A tempered chocolate is smooth, shiny and it has a snap when broken. If you have tempered chocolate right it will set in 5 minutes.
   The different types of chocolate—dark, milk or white —have different temperature characteristics.

4. **Nappe:** A French culinary term used to indicate the consistency of a sauce or custard. Here is how: the sauce has reached the right consistency, if you run a spoon on the wall of the pot, and the spoon leaves a clear path showing the thickness of the sauce or custard that does not run, but holds its shape and silkiness.

5. **Levain:** It is a French term for a sourdough culture or starter to make breads. A sourdough culture
   has many beneficial nutritional microorganisms just like in a yogurt, but this is found in grains. A culture improves the flavor of breads and texture. The breads made with a sourdough (levain) will have light to strong flavor profiles depending on the grains used and aging of the culture.

Index

About the Author

Jeannette Werle is a certified integrated health coach in Ohio where she sees clients and works in recipe development to meet her client's needs. She is married and has two grown sons. She received culinary training from many prestigious schools inside and outside the United States. In addition, she was the founder of a small bakery in Ohio which she ran for about 25 years and sold in 2018. Jeannette also has an extensive background in dental field which came from being in a private dental practice as a registered dental hygienist.

www.ingramcontent.com/pod-product-compliance
Lightning Source LLC
LaVergne TN
LVHW070215110826
845147LV00003B/580

9780578702490